Albert Einstein

Top 56 Inspirational and Educational Lessons that will Awaken You

Mark Wasilweska

Table of Contents

Introduction   5

Chapter 1: 56 inspirational and educational lessons   7

1. Live for today   7
2. Learn from the past   7
3. Hope for the future   7
4. Believe in action   7
5. Alter your thoughts to solve problems   7
6. Apply your brain   8
7. Don't get lazy in your thinking   8
8. Always be curious   8
9. Gain experience in your life   8
10. Never stop questioning   8
11. Have a strong attitude   8
12. Don't be afraid to commit mistakes   9
13. Try to be useful for others   9
14. Imagine   9
15. Try to be creative in your thinking   9
16. Keep moving ahead in life   9
17. Find a balance in your life   10
18. Treat everything as a miracle   10
19. You should be ready for opposition   10

20. Enjoy the mystery of life	10
21. Seek joy in creative expression	10
22. Understand the difference between information and knowledge	10
23. Seek joy from nature	11
24. Try to be a person of value	11
25. Reflect deeply	11
26. Understand the power of experimentation	11
27. Explain things in simple way	11
28. Understand things	11
29. Try new things	11
30. More importance to imagination and not knowledge	12
31. You should be passionate about things	12
32. Understand your problems well	12
33. Work tirelessly	12
34. Enjoy the monotony of a quiet life	12
35. Understand things the way they are	13
36. Save yourself from over confidence	13
37. Don't take praises too seriously	13
38. Learn to give	13
39. Don't overthink about things	13
40. Don't fret about the future	13
41. You should be trustworthy	14
42. You should follow the path of truth	14
43. Accept your shortcomings	14
44. Don't ignore your limitations	14
45. Work hard to overcome your limits	14

46. You should be humble	14
47. Focus on your capacity to learn	15
48. Don't get discouraged by things that you don't know about	15
49. Practice acceptance	15
50. Don't get pressurised by your social environment	15
51. Take things as they come	15
52. Understand that the universe is infinite	15
53. Don't overestimate your intelligence	16
54. See yourself in accordance with the nature	16
55. Look at new possibilities	16
56. Never force peace on anyone	16
Conclusion	**17**

Your Free Gift

I am really grateful and thankful for your purchase. As a small symbol of my appreciation, I would like to give you my FREE book on how to manage your time more efficiently to help you in your life.

In my time management ebook, you will find various ways and methods that will help you take control of your time and hence become more productive, so you can get more done in your day. You will also get all my new ebooks at a discounted price ☺

Here is the link for the ebook:

Download Now

Introduction

Albert Einstein was a German scientist. He is popular for his theory of relativity. He was a renowned physicist, writer, philosopher and thinker. He is credited with some very important inventions. He successfully applied philosophy to scientific inventions. Many successful people all over the world credit him with providing insightful advice on how to lead a successful and fruitful life.

Albert Einstein led a life that can be an inspiration for many. He was a great thinker. He always tried to improve the quality of his work and life. His popular teachings have helped many people to understand the basics of being successful and effective. These lessons can help you to look at your life in a new light. You can attain great heights by following these golden rules. His experience has taught many people the right ways to lead an effective and successful life.

He was a disciplined man who led his life in the most fruitful and effective manner. His life can be an inspiration of millions even today. Anyone can follow his teachings to lead a happy and effective life. The lessons are easy to follow.

Here, I am going to share some exceptional life changing teachings and lessons of Albert Einstein, which will help you to achieve more in your life.

You can apply his teachings and lessons in your everyday life to get the maximum benefits.

Chapter 1: 56 inspirational and educational lessons

1. Live for today

You should always live for your today. While it is important to learn from the past, it is equally important to live for the present. If you live for your today, you put in all your efforts to make your present better. This will help you to live a simple, yet effective life. You will notice how you are able to complete more number of tasks in the same number of hours. You should always live in the present.

2. Learn from the past

While it is important to live in the present, it is equally important to learn from the past. Your past achievements can motivate you to achieve more in your life. Your past failures can teach you how you can overcome your shortcomings. It is extremely important that you learn your lessons well from your past. Your past can help you to be a better person and can also help you to achieve more in your present and your future.

3. Hope for the future

You should always strive to improve the quality of your life. It is important that you hope for a better future and work towards it. You should always hope for a future that is happy and better.

4. **Believe in action**

If you wish to improve your life, you should believe in your actions. You should always try to work hard to achieve what you want to achieve. Nothing is impossible to achieve if you believe in your actions. Your actions should justify your thoughts and your aim in life.

5. **Alter your thoughts to solve problems**

You can't expect to solve your issues and problems if you don't alter the way you think and function. It is important that you alter the way you think, so that you can successfully solve all your problems.

6. **Apply your brain**

No matter what you achieve in your life, you should apply your brain into it. You should be involved actively in whatever it is that you are trying to achieve. You should always try to apply your brain to everything that you are doing. This will also help you to improve your experience and will also enhance the quality of your work. Your brain has immense power that you should apply to your life.

7. **Don't get lazy in your thinking**

You should not get into the habit of being so mechanical with your work, that you get lazy in the way you think. There are many people who follow set patterns and in the process get very lazy in the way they think. You should avoid getting into such a pattern. You should make sure that you actively use the power of your brain into your daily life. You should make sure that you are not lazy in your thinking.

8. **Always be curious**

A person who is curious by nature achieves much more on a daily basis as compared to the person who is not curious. You should always maintain a level of curiosity in your life. You need to be curious about things around you. This will help you to add a lot of value in your daily life.

9. **Gain experience in your life**

You should always try to gain more and more experience in your life. You can't make up for the lack of experience in your life with anything else. So, it is important that you relentlessly work towards your goal. This will help you to improve in your work by gaining more experience. The more experience you have in your life, the more you can judge what is right for you and what is not.

10. **Never stop questioning**

If you want to succeed in your life, you should always question things around you. You should never give up questioning if you want to grow as an individual. A person who thinks and imagines a lot will ask a lot of questions. This will help you to understand things around you in a better way and also from different perspectives. You should always allow yourself to be question things around you.

11. Have a strong attitude

A person with a good attitude will always have a good character. If you don't invest your time in building a strong attitude in your life, then your efforts to improve other aspects of your life might just get wasted. So, it is important that you develop a strong attitude in your life.

12. Don't be afraid to commit mistakes

If you wish to excel in everything that you do in your life, then you should never be afraid of making mistakes. A person who commits mistakes is someone who tries new things in his life. You should always look for an opportunity to try something new in your life.

13. Try to be useful for others

You will feel happy and accomplished if you try to make yourself useful for others. You can make your life purposeful, if you live for others. It is important that you understand simple ways that you can apply each day of your life to be helpful to others. When you try to be useful to others, you create a purpose in your life. This purpose will help you to be a better person and live a better life.

14. Imagine

A person should always use the power of imagination in his life. Your thoughts can change your life. If you wish to see positive changes in your life, you should understand the importance and power of imagination.

Your thoughts can attract good things in your life. So, it is only relevant and important that you use the power of imagination to make your life better in every way.

15. **Try to be creative in your thinking**

You should understand the importance of your thoughts. You thoughts have the power to mould your life. So, it is extremely important that you give due importance to the way you think. You should always try to be more creative in the way you think. This will help you to understand things from different perspectives. This simple act will bring wonders in your life.

16. **Keep moving ahead in life**

The only way to lead a successful life is to keep moving ahead in your life. You need to understand that you can never lead a happy and successful life, until and unless you look and ahead and move forward. It is extremely important that you learn from your past mistakes and apply the lessons that you have learnt in future. This will help you to achieve more success and happiness in your life.

17. **Find a balance in your life**

You should always look for a balance in your life. You should understand the importance of moderation in your daily rituals. When you find a balance within in your life, you will feel energised and motivated to achieve much more in your life. No matter what you do in your life, you should always look for a balance in your life.

18. **Treat everything as a miracle**

Things are always the way you see and view them. If you think that nothing is a miracle, then you will not see any miracle in your life. But, when you decide to find miracle in everything, you will find miracles all around. The best way that a person can choose is to treat everything in his life as a miracle. You should find miracles in the smallest of things.

19. **You should be ready for opposition**

Great and different people have always had to face opposition from people who can't think and function like them. If you have the gift of a great mind, then you have to be prepared for opposition from people who don't have such a mind. You should not be shocked when you meet such people in your life. You should always be prepared for such people.

20. **Enjoy the mystery of life**

You should always enjoy your life as it is. Life by nature is full of mystery. The best way to deal with this mystery is to enjoy it. You need to accept that your life will always have some mystery, no matter how much you try to figure it out. Always be aware of this mystery also try to enjoy it the way it is.

21. **Seek joy in creative expression**

If you wish to improve the quality of your life, you should find joy in creative expression. You should try to be creative in everything that you do with your life. This will help you to express yourself better and will also give you immense happiness and joy.

22. Understand the difference between information and knowledge

You should understand the difference between information and knowledge. You should understand the power of knowledge and should always strive to gain more knowledge in your life. You should also know how you perceive information in your life.

23. Seek joy from nature

You should also derive pleasure and happiness form nature. You should spend some quality time in nature and should understand its importance and significance in your life.

24. Try to be a person of value

While you should try to achieve more and more in your life, you should also try to be a person of value. A person of value will always add more value to things around him.

25. Reflect deeply

If you want to achieve more in your life, you will have to give importance to the process of deep reflection. When you can reflect on things at a deeper level, you can understand them well.

26. **Understand the power of experimentation**

You should always give importance to experimentation in your life. This will help you to understand things well and also explore them well. To make your life simple and rewarding, you should always believe in experimentation. This will help you a lot.

27. **Explain things in simple way**

If you understand things well, you will be able to explain them in simple words. You should always try to explain everything in the simplest of ways. If you can't explain something in a simple way, it means that you haven't understood it well.

28. **Understand things**

You should be more inquisitive as a person. It is important that you understand things around you. When you are able to do this, you will be able to enhance the quality of your life. You should understand things on a deeper level.

29. **Try new things**

It is important that you try new things in your life. This will help you to get a new perspective of things and will also help you to achieve the standard of your life. You should alter the way you think to see things in a better light.

30. **More importance to imagination and not knowledge**

While knowledge is important, you should also understand that imagination is more important than knowledge. There is immense power in imagination. When you can imagine great things in your life, you will also be able to achieve them. So, you should always give more importance to imagination.

31. **You should be passionate about things**

You should be passionate about things that you choose to do in life. This is important if you want to see positive results in your life. You should be passionate about the things that you do, be it work or otherwise. When you are passionate about everything that you do in your life, you will notice that you will be able to achieve much more than you had set out to.

32. **Understand your problems well**

You should acknowledge the challenges that you face in your life. This will help you to deal with them effectively. You should understand the nature of your problems and should address them. There is no point in ignoring your issues. You should face them and should find out ways to solve them.

33. **Work tirelessly**

You can lead a happy life if you commit yourself to your work. You should pledge to work tirelessly in the direction of your work. When you devote yourself to your work, you will not waste your precious time on less important things. You need to work hard consistently if you wish to achieve your goals.

34. **Enjoy the monotony of a quiet life**

There are many people that are scared of the monotony of a quiet life. You should not abhor this monotony. In fact, you should find peace in this monotony. When you learn to work under the comfort of this monotony, your life will improve in every respect. This is a simple yet effective way to improve the quality of your life.

35. **Understand things the way they are**

You should not try to mould things as per your convenience. You should always try to understand things the way they are. When you mould things as per your convenience, you completely lose the purpose of doing that thing. You should learn to accept things in your life for what they are. This acceptance will help you in many ways in your work and in general life also.

36. **Save yourself from over confidence**

You should always avoid over confidence to get the better of you. A person who is over confident will not be able to achieve to the best of his potential. It is important to be confident in whatever you choose to do. But, you should always be careful and should avoid falling in the trap of over confidence.

37. **Don't take praises too seriously**

There might be many people who would praise you for your efforts and achievements in your life. Though it is important to acknowledge these praises and the people, but you should not take these praises too seriously. You should know where to draw a line. When you take such things very seriously, there is always the risk of getting distracted from your path.

38. **Learn to give**

You should learn to give as a human being. A person who knows how to give to others will always be happy. Such a person does not expect much from anyone and believes in his own hard work. You should be giving n your nature. Always try to give more in your work and in your life.

39. **Don't overthink about things**

If you want to improve the quality of your life, you should abstain from the bad habit of overthinking. There are many people who multiply their problems just by overthinking about them. When you think too much, you lose the energy to focus in the right direction. Instead of overthinking, you should focus on the right things.

40. **Don't fret about the future**

You need to be hopeful about your future and should also prepare for your future. But, there is no point in fretting about the future. If you get too much worried about your future, you will not be able to concentrate on your present. This will mean that your attention and resources are divided amongst things that are wasting them.

41. **You should be trustworthy**

You should be a trustworthy person. No matter what you achieve in your professional life, you can't be truly happy unless you are a trustworthy person. You need establish a relationship of trust with everyone you work with. This will have a huge positive impact on your life.

42. **You should follow the path of truth**

It is not always easy to follow the path of truth, but you should relentlessly follow the path of truth. The best way to be on this path is to be truthful even in the smallest of matters. You should try to follow this simple mantra in your life.

43. **Accept your shortcomings**

You will have many shortcomings. You can't escape them. You need to accept that you are a human being, and like all human beings you are bound to have many shortcomings. You can only improve and make your life better if you are ready to accept your shortcomings as a person.

44. Don't ignore your limitations

You will face many difficulties in your professional as well as personal life. You will also have to face your limitations. If you choose to ignore these issues and limitations, you will make your life difficult. If you want to lead a happy life then accept all the challenges and limitations that come your way.

45. Work hard to overcome your limits

The only way to overcome your limits is to accept their existence and to work hard on them. You can achieve anything if you focus and decide to work hard.

46. You should be humble

No matter where you stand in your life, you should never forget to be humble. A humble person can achieve much more that a normal person. You should follow this in your life.

47. Focus on your capacity to learn

There are many people who waste too much time thinking about things they can't accomplish. You should always focus on your ability to learn things. When you focus on the right things, you will get the right results. You need to pay attention to the areas where you can grow.

48. Don't get discouraged by things that you don't know about

There could be many things that you don't understand. Such things can intimidate you. You should never waste your time feeling discouraged or intimidated by events. In fact, you should focus all your energies on how you can improve as a person. This will help you to reap great benefits from your life.

49. Practice acceptance

You should always be accepting in nature. You should accept things for what they are. This point will help you to divert your energies in the right direction.

50. Don't get pressurised by your social environment

A person's social environment can pull him down in many ways. You should never get pressurised by your social environment. You should only allow your environment to affect you in positive ways.

51. Take things as they come

You should be fearless when it comes to living your life your way. You should take things as and when they come up in your life. There is no point in getting tensed about something that hasn't even happened.

52. Understand that the universe is infinite

You should always consider your experience in comparison to the universe. The universe is vast and infinite. When you allow yourself to enjoy this realization, you will notice how humble and grateful you feel for your existence.

53. Don't overestimate your intelligence

You should believe in yourself, but there is no point in being overconfident about anything. If you wish to live a life of worth, you need to remember that you shouldn't overestimate yourself. You should be confident about yourself, but you should know where to draw the line.

54. See yourself in accordance with the nature

A person should always see himself in accordance with nature. This realization will help you to give your best in whatever you do in your life. You should look at nature for seeking inspiration and to perform better in your life in all aspects.

55. Look at new possibilities

You should always be on the lookout of new possibilities in your life. These possibilities will bring new challenges. You should always be ready for new adventures that are waiting for you.

56. Never force peace on anyone

Peace can only be understood and accepted. It can never be forced. You should never try to force peace on anyone. This will defeat the whole purpose of peace.

Conclusion

Albert Einstein was a great physicist, inventor and philosopher of his times. He led a disciplined life and used philosophy in science. His teachings are relevant even in today's world. He led his life in a simple yet effective manner. His educational teachings and lessons are so useful and practical that anyone can use them to transform their life for the better.

It is very important that a person understands how he can add value in his life and in his work. This will help him to be more productive and will also allow him to work more towards things that he truly values. You need to understand some basic points if you are looking to lead a simple yet effective way. You need to work towards making your daily life more productive and effective.

In this book, you will discover 56 important and effective educational lessons from Albert Einstein. These lessons will help you to transform your life for the better and will also help you to lead a more fruitful and happy life. These lessons are simple to understand. They will help you can form a framework for you, on which you can create a strong structure for your work life and your daily regular life.

Good luck!

Your Free Gift

I am really grateful and thankful for your purchase. As a small symbol of my appreciation, I would like to give you my FREE book on how to manage your time more efficiently to help you in your life.

In my time management ebook, you will find various ways and methods that will help you take control of your time and hence become more productive, so you can get more done in your day. You will also get all my new ebooks at a discounted price ☺

Here is the link for the ebook:

Download Now

Printed in Great Britain
by Amazon